THE ROYAL COURT THEATRE PRESENTS

The Woods

by Robert Alan Evans

The Woods was first performed at the Royal Court Jerwood Theatre
Upstairs, Sloane Square, on Wednesday 5 September 2018.

The Woods
by Robert Alan Evans

CAST (in alphabetical order)

Boy **Finn Bennett**
Kid/Hospital Porter **Charles Furness**
Wolf **Tom Mothersdale**
Woman **Lesley Sharp**

Director **Lucy Morrison**
Designer **Naomi Dawson**
Lighting Designer **Anthony Arblaster**
Music & Sound Designer **Tom Gibbons**
Movement Director **Vicki Igbokwe**
Assistant Director **Natasha Kathi-Chandra**
Casting Director **Amy Ball**
Production Manager **Marty Moore**
Costume Supervisor **Gina Lee**
Stage Managers **Naomi Buchanan Brooks,
Laura Draper, Julia Slienger**
Stage Manager Work Placement **Millie Bobanovic**

The Royal Court & Stage Management wish to thank the following for their help with this production:
Mel Kenyon, Adam Lawler, Doctor Miele, Rachel Taylor, Jamael Westman, Owen Whitelaw,
Thomas Williams, The Young Vic.

The Woods
by Robert Alan Evans

Robert Alan Evans (Writer)

For the Royal Court: **A Girl in a Car with a Man.**

Other theatre includes: **Kes (Leeds Playhouse/ Catherine Wheels); The River & the Mountain (LAMDA); Peter Pan (Sherman Cymru); Ignition (National Theatre of Scotland); Mikey & Addie (2012 Cultural Olympiad); The Voice Thief, Caged, Pobby & Dingan, Pondlife, Kappa (Catherine Wheels); Pinocchio [adaptation] (Royal & Derngate, Northampton); Mr Snow, The Night Before Christmas (Leeds Playhouse/ MacRobert Arts Centre); Beautiful Cosmos (Tron).**

Radio includes: **The Cracks.**

As director, theatre includes: **Crumble's Search for Christmas, Mr Snow (Leeds Playhouse/ MacRobert Arts Centre); Aruba, Fish Story (People Can Run); Naked Neighbour Twitching Blind (Tramway).**

As writer/director, dance includes: **Little Red, Tiger, Tiger Tale (Barrowland Ballet/Tramway).**

As co-writer, television includes: **Thieving Bastards, Get Together, Passengers.**

Awards include: **Critics' Awards for Theatre in Scotland (The Voice Thief); TMA Award for Best Show for Children & Young People (Pobby & Dingan); Prix d'Orpheon Award (Simon la Gadouille).**

Robert is currently part of the European PUSH project to experiment with gender and sexuality in work for young people.

Anthony Arblaster
(Lighting Designer)

Theatre includes: **Shadows of Time (Marysas Trio); Town Hall Cherubs (BAC).**

Opera includes: **Kettlehead, The Viagron, Women Box (Size Zero Opera).**

As associate lighting designer, theatre includes: **Woyzeck in Winter (Galway International Arts Festival/ Barbican); Mrs Henderson Presents (West End/ Toronto).**

As associate lighting designer, dance includes: **The Knot, The Happiness Project (Didy Veldman/ Umanoove).**

As associate lighting designer, opera includes: **Der Fliegende Holländer, Tristan und Isolde, Der Ring des Nibelungen (Longborough Festival).**

Finn Bennett (Boy)

Television includes: **Kiri, Liar, Cider with Rosie, Top Boy 2.**

The Woods is Finn's professional stage debut.

Naomi Dawson (Designer)

For the Royal Court: **Men in the Cities (& Traverse/ UK tour).**

Other theatre includes: **As You Like It (Regent's Park Open Air); Happy Days (Royal Exchange, Manchester); The Duchess of Malfi, Doctor Faustus, The White Devil, The Roaring Girl, As You Like It, King John (RSC); The Winter's Tale (Romateatern, Gotland); The Tin Drum (Kneehigh/Liverpool Everyman/West Yorkshire Playhouse); Beryl (West Yorkshire Playhouse/ UK tour); Much Ado About Nothing (Rose, Kingston); Kasimir & Karoline, Fanny & Alexander, Love & Money (Malmö Stadsteater, Sweden); Every One (BAC); Weaklings (Warwick Arts Centre); Hotel, Three More Sleepless Nights (National); Wildefire, Belongings, The Gods Weep (Hampstead); Brave New World, Dancing at Lughnasa, In Praise of Love (Royal & Derngate, Northampton); Monkey Bars (Unicorn/Traverse); Landscape & Monologue (Ustinov, Bath); Amerika, Krieg der Bilder (Staatsheater Mainz, Germany); Scorched (Old Vic Tunnels); Mary Shelley, The Glass Menagerie, Speechless (Shared Experience); The Typist (Sky Arts); King Pelican, Speed Death of the Radiant Child (Drum, Plymouth); If That's All There Is (Lyric, Hammersmith); ...Sisters (& Headlong), State of Emergency, Mariana Pineda (Gate); Stallerhof, Richard III, The Cherry Orchard, Summer Begins (Southwark Playhouse); Attempts on Her Life, Widows, Touched (BAC); Home, In Blood, Venezuela, Mud, Trash (Arcola); The Container, Phaedra's Love, The Pope's Wedding, Forest of Thorns (Young Vic).**

Opera includes: **Madama Butterfly, The Lottery, The Fairy Queen (Bury Court Opera); Madama Butterfly (Arcola).**

Charles Furness
(Kid/Hospital Porter)

Theatre includes: **Black & White, As You Like It (NYT); Isaac Came Home from the Mountain (Theatre503).**

Television includes: **The Enfield Haunting, The Passing Bells, 24: Live Another Day, Jamaica Inn, Silent Witness, Sherlock, The Whale.**

Film includes: **The Sense of an Ending.**

Tom Gibbons
(Music & Sound Designer)

For the Royal Court: **Goats, Love Love Love.**

Other theatre includes: **Oedipus (Toneelgroep, Amsterdam); The Lorax (Old Vic); Venus In Fur (West End); Hamlet (Almeida/West End); Oresteia (Almeida/Trafalgar Studios); Mr Burns, 1984 (Almeida/West End/Broadway); A View from the Bridge (& West End), Life of Galileo, Happy Days, A Season in the Congo, Disco Pigs (Young Vic); Hedda Gabler, Sunset at the Villa Thalia, The Red Barn, People Places & Things (National/West End); Les Misérables (Wermland Opera, Sweden); The Crucible (Broadway); Anna Karenina (Royal Exchange, Manchester); The Moderate Soprano, Elephants (Hampstead); White Devil, As You Like It (RSC); Translations, Plenty (Crucible, Sheffield); The Absence of War, Romeo & Juliet (Headlong); Lion Boy (Complicite); Henry IV, Julius Caesar (Donmar/ St Ann's, Brooklyn); Grounded (Gate); The Spire (Salisbury Playhouse); The Sound of Heavy Rain, The Initiate, Our Teacher's a Troll (& National Theatre of Scotland); Lungs, London, The Angry Brigade, Wasted (Paines Plough); The Rover (Hampton Court Palace); Dead Heavy Fantastic (Liverpool Everyman); Chalet Lines, The Knowledge, Little Platoons, Fifty Ways to Leave Your Lover (Bush).**

Awards include: **Olivier Award for Best Sound Design (People, Places & Things).**

Vicki Igbokwe (Movement Director)

As creative director/choreographer, dance includes: **Our Mighty Groove (UK tour); The Head Wrap Diaries (Tour).**

As mass movement choreographer, live events include: **London 2012 Olympic & Paralympic opening & closing ceremonies; Sochi 2014 Olympic & Paralympic opening & closing ceremonies; Glasgow 2014 Commonwealth Games opening ceremony; 2017 Azerbaijan Islamic Solidarity Games opening & closing ceremonies.**

Vicki is a creative director, choreographer and founder of Uchenna, a dance company based in London. She is a trustee for One Dance UK, the UK body for dance, and an Associate Artist at The Place.

Natasha Kathi-Chandra
(Assistant Director)

As director, theatre includes: **Om Shanti F*ck, The Infinite Line Between Dating & Dying [& writer], Symbiosis (Namashkar Arts); Voices of the Movement (Park); Mummy Dearest (Tabard).**

As assistant director, theatre includes: **The House of In Between (Theatre Royal Stratford East); Women of Hope (Arora Arts).**

Natasha is a writer and director. She founded her youth theatre company Ingenium Dramatics in her hometown in India at age seventeen.

Lucy Morrison (Director)

For the Royal Court: **Lights Out/It's All Made Up/The Space Between (The Site Programme), MANWATCHING, Plaques & Tangles, Live Lunch Series, Who Cares, Pests, Product (& Clean Break/Traverse/European tour).**

Other theatre includes: **Elephant (Birmingham Rep); Billy the Girl, This Wide Night (Clean Break/Soho); Little on the Inside (Clean Break/ Almeida/Latitude); it felt empty when the heart went at first but it is alright now (Clean Break/ Arcola); Fatal Light, Doris Day (Soho).**

Lucy is Associate Director at the Royal Court.

Tom Mothersdale (Wolf)

Theatre includes: **John, Cleansed (National); Oil (Almeida); The Glass Menagerie, Boys, Romeo & Juliet (Headlong); Crave, 4.48 Psychosis (Crucible, Sheffield); The Cherry Orchard (Young Vic); In Lambeth (Southwark); Missing Dates (Hampstead); King Lear (BAM, NYC/ Chichester Festival); Thursday (Adelaide International Festival); The Revenger's Tragedy (Independent Productions); Iphigenia, Pride & Prejudice (Theatre, Royal Bath); An Ideal Husband (West End); The Comedy of Errors (Globe); A Thousand Stars Explode in the Sky (Lyric, Hammersmith).**

Television includes: **Hanna, Philip K Dick's Electric Dreams: The Hood Maker, Doc Martin, King Charles III, Endeavour, Peaky Blinders.**

Film includes: **Overlord, Unseen, The Rain Collector, Actress.**

Awards include: **Ian Charleson Award (The Cherry Orchard).**

Lesley Sharp (Woman)

For the Royal Court: **Ingredient X, Top Girls (& UK tour), Our Country's Good, Greenland, Road, Shirley, Gone, Who Knew McKenzie.**

Other theatre includes: **The Seagull (Lyric, Hammersmith); A Taste of Honey, Harper Regan, Mother Courage, Uncle Vanya, Murmuring Judges, Six Characters in Search of an Author, Fathers & Sons, Tin Tang Mine, True Dare Kiss, Command or Promise (National); Ghosts, Little Voice (West End); God of Hell, A Family Affair (Donmar); Playing With Trains, Mary & Lizzie (RSC); Summerfolk (Chichester Festival).**

Television includes: **Living the Dream, Three Girls, Paranoid, Scott & Bailey, Capital, Starlings, The Shadow Line, Whistle & I'll Come to You, Cranford, Poirot, The Diary of Anne Frank, Red Riding, Doctor Who, The Children, Afterlife, Carrie's War, The Second Coming, Bob & Rose, Clocking Off, Nature Boy, Great Expectations, Common As Muck, Dandelion Dead, Frank Stubbs, Road, Top Girls, Born with Two Mothers.**

Film includes: **Dusty & Me, Inkheart, Vera Drake, Cheeky, From Hell, The Full Monty, Naked, Priest, Close My Eyes, The Rachel Papers, Rita Sue & Bob Too, The Love Child.**

Awards include: **Sky Arts Television Award for Best Actress, Golden Nymph Award for Outstanding Actress in a Drama Series (Afterlife); Broadcasting Press Guild Award for Best Actress (Bob & Rose); Broadcasting Press Guild Award for Best Actress (Clocking Off); SAG Award for Outstanding Performance by a Cast (The Full Monty); Award for Outstanding Performance by a Cast (The Full Monty).**

THE ROYAL COURT THEATRE

The Royal Court Theatre is the writers' theatre. It is a leading force in world theatre for energetically cultivating writers – undiscovered, emerging and established.

Through the writers, the Royal Court is at the forefront of creating restless, alert, provocative theatre about now. We open our doors to the unheard voices and free thinkers that, through their writing, change our way of seeing.

Over 120,000 people visit the Royal Court in Sloane Square, London, each year and many thousands more see our work elsewhere through transfers to the West End and New York, UK and international tours, digital platforms, our residencies across London, and our site-specific work. Through all our work we strive to inspire audiences and influence future writers with radical thinking and provocative discussion.

The Royal Court's extensive development activity encompasses a diverse range of writers and artists and includes an ongoing programme of writers' attachments, readings, workshops and playwriting groups. Twenty years of the International Department's pioneering work around the world means the Royal Court has relationships with writers on every continent.

Within the past sixty years, John Osborne, Samuel Beckett, Arnold Wesker, Ann Jellicoe, Howard Brenton and David Hare have started their careers at the Court. Many others including Caryl Churchill, Athol Fugard, Mark Ravenhill, Simon Stephens, debbie tucker green, Sarah Kane – and, more recently, Lucy Kirkwood, Nick Payne, Penelope Skinner and Alistair McDowall – have followed.

The Royal Court has produced many iconic plays from Lucy Kirkwood's **The Children** to Jez Butterworth's **Jerusalem** and Martin McDonagh's **Hangmen**.

Royal Court plays from every decade are now performed on stage and taught in classrooms and universities across the globe.

It is because of this commitment to the writer that we believe there is no more important theatre in the world than the Royal Court.

Supported using public funding by
**ARTS COUNCIL
ENGLAND**

ROYAL

COMING UP AT THE ROYAL COURT

21 Sep – 6 Oct

Poet in da Corner
By Debris Stevenson

Part of Represent, a series of artworks inspired by the Representation of the People Act 1918.

Co-commissioned by 14-18 NOW and the Royal Court Theatre, supported by Jerwood Charitable Foundation, in association with Nottingham Playhouse and Leicester Curve.

24 – 27 Oct

Trying It On
Written and performed by David Edgar

Presented by Warwick Arts Centre and China Plate.

25 Oct – 24 Nov

ear for eye
By debbie tucker green

Produced in association with Barbara Broccoli.

31 Oct – 17 Nov

Still No Idea
Lisa Hammond and Rachael Spence

with Improbable and the Royal Court Theatre.

28 Nov – 12 Jan

Hole
By Ellie Kendrick

Hole is part of the Royal Court's Jerwood New Playwrights programme, supported by Jerwood Charitable Foundation.

6 Dec – 26 Jan

The Cane
By Mark Ravenhill

Tickets from £12

royalcourttheatre.com

Sloane Square London, SW1W 8AS ⊖ Sloane Square
⇌ Victoria Station 🐦 royalcourt 🇫 royalcourttheatre

JERWOOD **CHARITABLE** FOUNDATION

ROYAL COURT SUPPORTERS

The Royal Court is a registered charity and not-for-profit company. We need to raise £1.5 million every year in addition to our core grant from the Arts Council and our ticket income to achieve what we do.

We have significant and longstanding relationships with many generous organisations and individuals who provide vital support. Royal Court supporters enable us to remain the writers' theatre, find stories from everywhere and create theatre for everyone.

We can't do it without you.

"There are no spaces, no rooms in my opinion, with a greater legacy o
fearlessness, truth and clarity than this space.

Simon Stephens, Associate Playwrigh

The Royal Court invests in the future of the theatre, offering writers the
support, time and resources to find their voices and tell their stories
asking the big questions and responding to the issues of the moment

As a registered charity, the Royal Court relies on the generous support o
individuals to seek out, develop and nurture new voices. Please join us in
Writing The Future by donating today

You can donate online at royalcourttheatre.com/donate or via our
donation box in the Bar & Kitchen

We can't do it without you

Writing the Future

**To find out more about the different
ways in which you can be involved
please contact
Charlotte Cole on 020 7565 5049 /
charlottecole@royalcourttheatre.com**

The English Stage Company at the Royal Court Theatre is a registered charity (No. 231242).

The Woods

Robert Alan Evans is a writer, director and devisor. He has written extensively for young people and co-created several dance pieces. Theatre includes *A Girl in a Car with a Man*, *Aruba*, *Fish Story*, *The Voice Thief*, *Caged*, *Pondlife*, *Mikey and Addie*, *The Dark*, *Kappa* and *The River and the Mountain*. His adaptations include *Kes*, *Peter Pan*, *Pinocchio*, *Pobby and Dingan* and *The Sleeping Beauties*. His collaboration with choreographers include *Tiger, Tiger Tale* and *Little Red*. He grew up outside Cardiff and has lived and worked in Edinburgh, Glasgow and now London.

also by Robert Alan Evans from Faber

A GIRL IN A CAR WITH A MAN

ROBERT ALAN EVANS

The Woods

ff

FABER & FABER

First published in 2018
by Faber and Faber Limited
74–77 Great Russell Street, London WC1B 3DA

Typeset by Country Setting, Kingsdown, Kent CT14 8ES
Printed in England by CPI Group (UK) Ltd, Croydon, Surrey CR0 44Y

A CIP record for this book is available from the British Library

ISBN 978-0-571-35131-2

2 4 6 8 10 9 7 5 3 1

The Woods was first performed at the Royal Court Theatre, London, on 5 September 2018. The cast, in alphabetical order, was as follows:

Boy Finn Bennett
Kid Charles Furness
Wolf Tom Mothersdale
Woman Lesley Sharp

Director Lucy Morrison
Design Naomi Dawson
Lighting Design Anthony Arblaster
Music and Sound Design Tom Gibbons
Movement Direction Vicki Igbokwe

Act One

ONE

Black.

A sound.

The breathing of a baby on a baby-monitor.

A kitchen strip-light flickers and comes on.

Distant, we see a room in a sealed glass box.

It is a perfectly normal kitchen.

But something has happened. One of the cupboards is open and the glasses have been pulled from it and lie smashed on the floor.

Also lying on the floor is a chair upended. A baby-monitor lies beside it, red light flickering.

TWO

We see a shape in the darkness that surrounds the sealed room. It is a Woman, watching. She is wearing normal clothes; light, summery. They are old now though. Dirtied and a little ragged.

She looks confused. She starts to move towards the glass box.

The lights go out and the room disappears.

The sound rises and gets loud, overpowering. It has transformed into a storm.

The wind rising in a great forest of trees.

We can hear them bending and straining.

Snow whips the air above.

Sleet flying through the night.

The Woman is battling against it. She pulls her cardigan and jacket closer round her.

She looks up. Panic etched on her face as a flash of

7

lightning lights her up. The crackle of a tree struck. Then black. A crack of thunder. We can hear the tree begin to topple. The groaning sound of roots ripped from earth.
It falls and falls and falls.

THREE

Lights up.
A shack in the woods.
It has wooden walls and a wooden floor.
It has been here a long time.
It is dilapidated.
It is dark.
The Woman stands exhausted. Wet.
Lying in a pile on the floor is a Boy, unconscious. So pale. He could be dead.
She stares at him.
A long time.
She breathes heavily.
She notices the door is open.
She goes and shuts it.
She stands there a long time, her head resting on the door, then pulls the wooden bolt across.

FOUR

Later.
The Boy has been moved, rolled over.
She is crouched, looking at him from a distance.

FIVE

Later.
The same positions.
She suddenly comes out of her trance.
There is a noise from outside.
A creaking of the shack.
She freezes, alert. It sounds like someone is on the
roof, but could just be snow moving.
It stops.
She looks back at the Boy.
It looks like he has moved.
She approaches to see if that's correct.
He moves again, a gasp for air.
She tries to sink into the shadows along the wall.
He starts to shiver.
He sees her and stretches out a hand.
She shakes her head.
He starts shivering violently.
Unsure, she approaches him.
She looks about, then takes off her own jacket.
She holds it out to him.
He is not looking.
She grunts.
He sees her.
He shivers.
She throws the jacket at him.
It sits on the floor next to him.
She makes another noise.
She concentrates and speaks. The first time in a long
time. Broken, and with a Southern US accent.

Woman Gotta . . .

She takes the jacket and holds it closer to him.
He suddenly grabs it and pulls it tight.

9

Hey!
    Mine.
    Hear?
    'S mine.

    He stares at her.

Stop.

    . . .
    Lookin'.

    . . .

    . . .
    What you looking at?
    Ain't nothing here.
    You tricking me.

    She has second thoughts about the jacket.

Give it.
    'S mine.

    She takes it off him.
        He doesn't stop her.

. . . What?

    He starts to shiver again.
        Fade.

SIX

Later.
    Darkness.
    She is standing just outside the door.
    Her jacket gone.
    She suddenly feels the cold and hugs herself.
    She notices this, her body.
    She slowly takes her hands away and looks at them.
    Sees them.

Then the sound of something in the dark. A scuffling.
She looks up, frightened.

From far away we hear the sound of a television; the
repeated loop of an old American movie.

A moment, then a very intense pain grips her, folds
her over.

She slowly falls to her knees.

She moans, but tries to keep the sound inside.

She finally falls still, curled up with the side of her
head resting against the ground, as if she were being
pushed into it.

The pain goes.

SEVEN

The shack.

She comes in.

Goes to the Boy who is lying on a makeshift bed with
the jacket over him.

Woman Get out!
Hear me?
Get out!
Had enough of your tricks.

The Boy doesn't move.
He looks unconscious.

Well?
What you waiting for?
Come on.

She grabs him.
Violently she pulls him to his feet.
He starts to move, groggy.
She takes him to the door and tries to disentangle
herself.

Stand up.
  I said stand up!

She keeps trying to stand him up.
  But he can't do it without her.
  It's almost comical, like a rag doll.
  Eventually she stops.
  He leans against her.
  His touch is painful to her.
  She slumps against the door frame with him.
  They slide till they are sitting.

You can't . . .
  I can't look after you.

He reaches out and searches for something.
  Takes her hand.
  She stares at it. Her hand in his.

You like ice.

EIGHT

The Woman is outside. She has a small armful of wood.
She is staring at the ground.
  She bends and picks up something buried in the snow.
  It is a child's nightlight, the cord hanging limp,
broken off.
  She looks at it strange.
  It flickers.
  She does not see the Wolf. Sitting. Watching her.
  He speaks like a character in an old movie. From the
Deep South.

Wolf What you doing?

She gets a shock and drops the wood and the lamp.
The bulb smashes.
  The wood goes everywhere.

Oops.

I give you a shock, old woman?

She starts to collect the wood up.
 *He watches her, then slowly raises his foot, puts it
against her arse and pushes.*
 She goes head first into the snow.
 He tries not to laugh. But he can't help it.

I sorry.
 I didn't –
 Only –
 You so funny there, in the snow like that.

She gets up and starts collecting up the wood.

Oh, don't be like that.

She ignores him.

I didn't expect you to fall like that.
 Be honest, I didn't expect to push you entirely.
 In fact.
 I don't know where it came from.
 I just see an ass, I can't resist. I got to push it. Make
it tumble.
 You know what I mean?
 Just because I could.
 And I've always thought that if I can do something,
then I should.
 Don't matter what it is.
 It could be jumping up, see. Like this.

He jumps.

See how good that made me look?
 I look so good doing any kind of physical thing.
 One of my charms.
 See I . . .
 Spontaneous.

I full of life.
I the one.
I the one thing that I am.
That's the one thing that I am.
And I . . .
Well, I love it.
I just love it.
Ain't no future.
Ain't no past.
I just here, now.
Kickin' your ass.

Oh, you so boring.
Jeez.
She don't say a thing.
Does she?
Do you?
I said.
DO YOU?!

She doesn't look at him.

You know today I thought about having a salad.
I really wanted a salad.
It would've had so many things in it.
It would've had things you don't normally associate
with a salad.
Like . . .
Like . . .
Fuck!
Like . . .
Well, they're green. And they sort of like . . . peas, but
they're not peas.
Oh what are they called?
What are they called?

She is silent.
He is on her now.

Huh?
  Mama?
  What are they called?
  Green, like peas, only not.

  Considering her.

What you doing anyway?

  She tries to get past him.
    He blocks her path.

You not yourself.

  He stares at her.
    For a long time.
    She will not look at him.

(*Considering.*) Wood.
  Why you want wood?
  Huh?

  She tries to get past.
    He blocks her way.

You so old.
  How old you now?
  Huh?

You don't even know, do you?
  I tell you.
  You been here forever.
  You know how long that is?
  Since always.
  You gonna hold me?
  Huh?
  You gonna hold me, Mama?

  He tries to get her to hold him in her arms.

That ain't it.
  That ain't it at all.

You gotta put your arms round me.
See.

He tries to pull her arm round him.

Like this.

Her arm falls. He tries again.

Like this.

It falls. He tries again.

Like this.

It falls. She is lifeless.

Mama?

Woman Don't call me that.

Wolf Why not? Gave birth to me, didn't you?

Woman . . .

He looks at her so closely.

Wolf You awake.
You very awake.
What you got?

Woman Nothing.

Wolf You hiding something.
I can tell.
That smell.
Like a sweet sort of odour.
What is that?

*He is sniffing her, almost licking her hands. He goes to
her belly.*

Here.
Smells like . . .
You got something for me? Your only son. Your one
and only. Your little boy. Your lovely little boy.

'Cause it is cold out here.
It is so cold.
And I am hungry.
You hear me, Mama?
I am so hungry.

Woman I said don't call me that.

She moves away from him.
He looks at her. Dangerous.

Wolf I know what wood for.
You wanting a fire.
Floor not good enough for you?
The floor, you lay there for long time.
Floor once was your saviour. Was all you wanted.
Couldn't get you off it.
And now? Now you all bouncing all over the place
collecting wood?
Thinking *you* can light a fire?
What's wrong with the floor?

She suddenly falls to her knees.

I said, the floor.

She falls lower.
He comes over and pushes her head to the floor. It
mirrors her position from earlier.

You like my new shoes?
What I like most is that they form themselves
seamlessly around my foot.
They like a second skin, these shoes.
I don't know what to call them though.
They not sneakers.
They not shoes.
They sort of like daps.
Yeah.
Kinda old-fashioned, right?

That word.
'Daps'.
'Do you like my new daps?'
'I got these new daps, they make me so happy.'
'Why, of course.'
'Why yes, of course.'
'Why, sure.'
'Oh yes. Surely.'
'Well, certainly. Of course. We must.'
'Oh yes. We must.'
'Oh we must.'
'Oh we must.'

He is crying now, almost. Is it pretend?

Why you so cruel to me?
Huh?
I just wanna be a good boy.
I just wanna be everything you wanted.
I just wanna make you happy.

He has lowered himself so that he can look into her eyes. Pleading.

And now you not even looking at me?
Mama?

She turns her head away.
He stands.

I know you got something.
I know it.
Some little bit of something.
But you mark my words.
You will fall.
Like you always do.
You will fail.
And when you do.
Only me gonna be there for you.
Pick you back up.

Toodle-pip.
　　Bye-bye now.
　　I love you.
　　I love you so much.
　　Oh I love you so much.
　　Oh I love you. I love you so much.
　　I can't wait. I just can't wait till we all together again.
　　I see you in the next encounter.
　　I see you in the next episode.
　　Where I will have different shoes.
　　And maybe a different look entirely.
　　I like a wolf in sheep's clothing.
　　But you know it be me.
　　Because of my smile.
　　That don't ever change.
　　See.
　　. . .
　　CAPERS!
　　I fucking love capers.
　　I just love them.
　　I just love love love . . .

He leaves.
　　The lamp flickers in the snow.

NINE

Back in the shack.
　　She has carefully placed the wood she has collected in a pile in the fireplace.
　　She is staring at it.

Woman You just gotta . . .
　　Simple.
　　This simple.
　　Just . . .

She doesn't know what to do next.
    She is stuck.

Fuck!

She smashes the pile she has made, scattering the wood.

See!
    Told you.
    I can't.
    'S all wet. 'S all shit.
    Making me go out like that.
    Do those things, when I fine. I fine here.

She gives up.
    A noise brings her out of herself.
    It is the Boy. He has something in his hands.
A lighter.
    He is sparking it.
    After a few attempts it lights.

Hey.
    Hey!
    Stop.

He gives her the lighter.
    She stares at it.

Where you get this?

He takes her hands and helps her to spark it.
    She is mesmerised.
    She looks at him and remembers something.
    She pulls up a part of the floor, searches around with her hand and lets out a little noise of triumph as she pulls out a bird's nest.

Look.
    It a nest.
    You heard that word? 'Nest'.
    Look.

She pulls out a bird skeleton.

These the little babies.
    Mama must've gone left them.
    Found it.
    See I very observant.
    Know these woods like the back of my hand.
    'S how I found you.
    Buried there, in the snow.
    I see you because you an unusual lump.
    Ain't a normal lump. 'S how I found you. Brought
you back.
    You remember that?
    You heavy, but I carried you.
    All by myself.

She looks at the nest.

Tried feeding them.
    But it's hard.
    I don't know what they like.
    This one cheep the longest.
    Cheep cheep.
    I thought maybe I see their spirits go up or something.
    You know.
    Fly through the ceiling.
    But it don't happen.
    Nothing there.
    . . .
    We use it.
    'S what I saved it for.
    We use it for . . .
    Kindling.
    That's what it called.
    This 'kindling'.

*She takes out the bird bones and puts them carefully
next to the fire.*

Then she looks at the nest, takes a few twigs from it and puts them in the fireplace.
  The Boy sparks the lighter again.

Wow!
  Careful.
  You got to be careful with that.
  Ain't a toy.
  I show you.

She takes the lighter and shows him how to light it.
  Then she sets light to the twigs.

(*Delighted.*) Shit.
  Shit.
  Look at that!
  Look!
  It a flame.
  Look!
  It on fire!
  Shit.
  It on fire.
  We done that.

The fire starts to burn.
  She realises it's going to go out.
  She puts the whole nest on.
  It takes.
  She realises it's going to need more wood.

Shit.

She looks about.
  She picks up some of the wood she collected.
  It's too wet.

Shit.

She looks about.
  She looks at the walls of the shack.

*She goes to one of the planks of wood and
considers it.*
She has second thoughts.
*Then looks at the Boy and pulls one of the
planks off.*

Worth it.
For you.
We got to keep you warm.

*She carefully adds the wood to the small fire.
The flames take hold.*

Look.
It a fire.
Look.
It all warm.
Feel it?
You feel that?

He nods.

He said I never feel that again.
But I do.
(*Shouting at the chimney.*) I do feel that.
I warm.
You hear! You see what I done?!
I WARM!

She looks at the Boy.
A moment.
*Then something drops down the chimney into the
fire.*
She is terrified.

Get it off.
Get it off.
Get it off me.

She is cowering on the floor.

She slowly gets up.
The Boy has picked something off the flames. An old bird.
She comes closer and looks at it.

. . . Just a bird.

She is staring at the bird.

Look at it.
    Dry as a cracker.
    Been up there a long time.
    You think she the mom?
    Got stuck up there.
    I didn't hear her.
    If she cried out.
    (*To the bird.*) I sorry. I never heard you.
    All alone like that.
    Old thing.

I put you here with the little ones.

There.
    All bones together.
    . . .
    You know there ain't no such thing as a soul.
    I tried to look for 'em.
    Babies ain't got no soul, little one.
    They just dead and gone.
    . . .
    I think that good.
    I think that good, don't you?
    When we gone we gone.
    Just the flies come for us.
    . . .
    Can't just stand here.
    Can't just stand here looking around.
    We gotta build this up.
    We gotta look after you.

Burn it hot.
That keep things out.
Keep things coming down the chimney.
Sneaks and –
Just –
We burn their tails and they fly away.
Blazing!
'S true. I read it. Can tell you all them stories about
that.

. . .

If you want.
You wanna stay?
With me?

He nods.

Okay.
We just got to keep the fire going.

Suddenly noticing and checking the door.

And we keep this closed.
We stay inside.
You hear me?

He nods.

(*Looking at the lock.*) Shit. This ain't gonna keep out
shit.

*She looks around and pulls a packing case over, then
violently rams it up against the door.*

There. We always keep this here. Got it?

He nods.

What I say?

Boy Keep this here.

Woman Good boy.

25

Then we safe.
Right?
You and me.
We safe.

Boy Safe.

*She looks at the fire. She takes another stick of wood
and throws it on.*
 The flames grow.

TEN

We see the Wolf has been watching.
 He looks older.
 He suddenly notices something on his shoe. A stain.
 He licks his thumb and tries to get rid of it.
 Rubbing harder and harder to get it off.
 He takes his shoe off. He rubs it harder and harder.
 He stops.
 The sound of ice cracking. A tree splits. A branch falls.
 The Wolf jumps. He scarpers.

ELEVEN

*We see the flicker of a white fluorescent strip-light
somewhere.*
 *Then we see the kitchen light up again. Sealed and far
away.*
 It is back in order.
 *There is a helium balloon, a little old now and starting
to wrinkle, tied to the back of the chair.*
 The baby-monitor is unbroken and on the table.
 *A pile of what looks like baby clothes, folded, sits on
the table.*
 The baby-monitor lights up.

TWELVE

The sound of a baby crying somewhere distant.
    Lights up.
    The shack.
    She is standing over the Boy as if she has just woken from a dream, disorientated.
    The Boy stirs, a bad dream.

Woman Shhh.
    Shhhh.
    Just the wind.
    Just the wind in the trees.

She hums a fragment of lullaby.
    He falls still again.
    She looks at him.

What's your name?

    . . .
    Mathew?

    . . .
    Is that it?
    My name is . . .
    My name is . . .

She stretches out a hand to stroke his hair.
    He opens his eyes.
    She pulls her hand back.

Sorry.
    I didn't . . .
    I was just looking at your hair.
    So soft.
    How d'you get hair like that?
    Must have been born with it.
    Were you?
    Your mother.

You got a mother?
You remember her?

He shakes his head.

'S okay.
You don't remember anything?

He shakes his head.

You're such a strange boy.
Never thought I'd have such a strange boy.
Here, I mean.
Like a family in a way. You and me.
You don't remember anything?

Boy I remember . . .

Woman Yes?

Boy Storm.

Woman Was a storm when you came here.

Boy That's where I was.
Where I first was.
After you called me.

Woman I didn't call you.

Boy Did.
I heard you calling me.
You said 'Mathew'.

Overwhelmed. She nods her head.

So I opened my eyes and it was a storm I was in.
You called me in the storm.
But I couldn't find you.
I thought, why did she call me and then this?
Cold.
Alone.
Were you playing?

. . .
You were playing with me.

Woman No.
What about a home?
You remember a home?

He turns away.

Hey. It's okay.
I'm just trying to help.
. . .
Hey.
You not looking at me now?
Is that it?
. . .

What?

Boy I'm home.
This is home.
Don't you want me here?

. . .

You don't want me here.

Woman No.
It's not that.
I just . . .

He takes her hand and puts it in his hair.

I just . . .

Boy I'm yours.

Lights out.

THIRTEEN

Lights up in the shack.
   There are holes in the walls now.
   She is working at something on the fire. A pan.
   Then pours out a bowl of soup from the pan and takes it to the Boy.
   During this scene she sometimes slips into a British accent.

Woman Hey.
   Hey, sleepy head.
   Made something for you.

   She props him up and goes to give him the bowl.
      He doesn't take it.

Don't you want it?
   I thought you'd be hungry.

   He takes her hand and brings the bowl to his mouth.

Hey.
   Hey.

   She produces a spoon.
      He looks at it.
      She takes the spoon, dips it in the soup.
      Then feeds him.
      He sips it from the spoon.
      She takes another spoonful.
      He eats it.

You like it?

   He nods.

Tried it myself.
   So I'd know it wasn't too hot.
   Or cold.
   Sometimes things are too hot for little ones.

Or too cold.
I know that.
You have to put your elbow in it.
But not with soup.
That'd be stupid.
I just tasted it.
You like it, huh?

He nods and eats.

I never use tins.
Tins bad for a boy.
Oh sometimes, I guess.
If it's a special occasion or it's raining and we get in
all wet from the rain. And you've been splashing in the
puddles and I've been carrying things. The shopping.
Maybe then, for a treat.
Light the fire.
Eat together.
Watch the rain.
Or just talk.
Yeah.
We'd just say things like
'How are you?'
Or no, because we already know that stuff.
We'd just say things that are things about noticing
things like . . .
'You cold?'
Or 'It's a horrible day, isn't it?'
Or . . . 'You growing out of that jumper. Need a new
one soon'.
'You a growing boy'.
. . .
You feed yourself now.

He takes the spoon and drops it.

'S okay.

She picks it up and goes to hand it back.

What? You don't want it now?
   Fine.

   She eats a spoonful of the soup herself.
      She offers him another spoonful.
      He refuses so she eats it herself.
      She gets another spoonful and goes to put it in her
   mouth.
      He stops her hand, takes the spoon and eats.

You're easy to fool.
   You know that?
   That's the oldest trick in the book and you fell for it.
   You're a bit stupid.

I was thinking earlier. Maybe we should do this place
up a bit.
   You know. Make something of it.
   I know it isn't much, but . . .
   Could make you a room.
   What do you think?

   He looks at her and lets some of the soup dribble out
   of his mouth.
      She laughs, a bit uncomfortably.

That's disgusting.
   Stop it.

   He lets more dribble out.
      She gets agitated.

(*Violently.*) I said STOP IT!

You don't want it, that's fine.
   I wouldn't have made it.
   Only you've got to be tidy. Understand?
   I'm not used to company.
   You're a difficult boy, you are.
   Difficult to look after.
   I mean look at this place.

It's a mess.
See!
A mess.
Never like this before you came.
Making me burn everything.
Always wanting it so warm.
I can't keep burning everything for you.
Is that what you want?
You want us to burn it all?
Huh?

He shakes his head.

Because then what?
Then what?
No. No. Nowhere. That's where we'd be.
He out there.
And he is . . .
He is so . . .
I've seen him do that and he is so . . .
So, I'm just trying to protect you.
You understand that, right?

He nods.

Hey. Hey.
No need to look so scared.
You've just got be good, yeah?
You be a good boy?

He nods.

'S all I want.
Because then it's fine.
Then it's all fine.
Not doing anything wrong.
Just want to keep you safe.
That's all.
That's all.

He takes a spoonful of the soup and eats it.

FOURTEEN

A baby crying, distant. But a little closer now.
  The shack, which is now pockmarked with holes.
  Night.
  The Woman is standing as if asleep on her feet.
  She looks older. Tired.
  The crying stops.
  She wakes with a start.
  She sees that the fire has nearly gone out.
  She moves quickly; she rips a plank of wood from the
walls of the shack.
  She adds it to the fire.
  She watches intensely as the flames take hold. Relief.
  There is a noise at the door.
  A tapping.
  She freezes.
  Another tapping.

Wolf Mama?
  Mama.
  Ain't you gonna let me in?

  She goes to the door.
    Hides next to it.
    We see the Wolf. He is in rags now. Thin and weak.

I know you there.
  Can see you.

  A finger suddenly pokes through the wall very close to
  where she is standing.
    She jumps.

Mama.

Woman Go away.

Wolf Please.

You gotta let me in.
I dying out here.
Mama?
You killing me.

He has put more of his hand through now.
  She has picked up a heavy piece of wood.

Mama?

Woman I said go away.
  I don't need you any more.

She brings down the wood on his hand.
  He howls.
  The Boy moves.
  She goes to him.

Shhhhh.
  Shhhhhhh.

The Wolf watches through the walls.
  *He growls and starts to limp away, then he stops
  and notices something in the snow. It is the nightlight
  from earlier. He picks it up and looks at it.*
  He sees more. A broken baby-monitor.
  He picks it up.
  He sees something else buried.
  *It is the helium balloon from earlier. Completely
  flat and crumpled up like rubbish.*
  *Another thing. He pulls it from the snow. It is a
  baby's cardigan. It is hand-knitted, dark green. On it
  are knitted basic white triangular trees.*
  He disappears.

FIFTEEN

The shack.
  It has almost completely gone. The walls stripped bare.
  Every last piece of wood has gone. There is just enough of the frame left for it to still be a shack.
  The Woman enters. She is carrying the Boy.
  He is soaking wet and weak.
  She lays him down.
  She takes her coat off and wraps it round the Boy, who is shivering.
  She tries to get the fire to light.

Woman Come on!
  Come on!
  FUCK!

  The Boy stirs.

I'm sorry.
  I'm sorry.
  Not you. Not you.

  He reaches inside his jacket and pulls out a stick he has collected.
    She puts it on the fire.
    It takes.

What were you doing?
  I told you to stay here.
  Shhh.
  Shhhhhh.

  He reaches into his jacket again.
    He pulls out something new.
    It is a Coke can.
    She looks at it.

You find this?

He nods.

You were cold.
 I guess you woke up, huh?
 And what?
 I was standing there.
 That it?
 I do that sometimes.
 I have to think.
 You go into the woods?

He nods.

You . . .
 You see anything? Or . . .
 No?
 No.
 Course you didn't
 Black, ain't it?
 Black in those woods.
 See I knew you'd gone in there because they gone
silent. The trees.
 Always silent, but this like the sound sucked away.
 So, I woke up and saw you gone.
 I knew it.
 Little trail to where you walked in.
 Black, ain't it?
 You didn't . . .?
 You feel anything?
 You feel the trees getting tight?
 They get tight, don't they?
 So of course, I followed you.
 I love you so much, Mathew.
 I followed you.
 I cried out
 'Mathew!'
 'Mathew!'
 Did you hear me?

Did you hear me crying out for you?

He shakes his head.

No. Course not.
 'Cause they take all the sound away, those trees.
 That's what they do.
 They're so thick your voice just gets sucked up by them.
 And they get tight, don't they?
 Tight round you?
 You feel that?
 You feel their branches on you?
 It's all I could think about.
 'S why I had to get to you.
 Those branches going into you.
 Going right down inside you, don't they?
 They go right inside and crawl right through you.
 I know that be happening to you.
 You're so small.
 So little.
 See, I tried once.
 Tried to leave here.
 Tried to get out.
 Only there's no way.
 There's no way out.
 You just walk and walk and walk.
 And eventually you can't tell night from day.
 Or up from down.
 You can't tell anything.
 You have nothing.
 That's what they do.
 They leave you with nothing.
 You know that now.
 You know it.
 I know you know.
 We got to stay here.
 Because at least it's safe.

At least it's warm.
Warmer.
No.
We got to stay here.
Don't remember the last time.
Think I walked for days.
Weeks.
Then I must've heard –
Must've heard some kind of noise.
Like a bird calling.
Or maybe I saw glimmer of light.
Just a glimmer in all those trees, so black.
So of course I follow it.
And it brings me back here.
See.
It brings me back here.
The only place with any light.
See, I know this place like the back of my hand.
I know this very wooden little shack.
I know it's mine.
And I know it's yours.
And I know that.
We know it.
We've just got to stay.
Just stay.
Don't think about going.
Don't think about the rest.
Just you and me.

He tries to say something.

What's that?
  What?

Boy Cold.

Woman It's not so cold.
  I'll make you some of my soup.

Hey?
You like that?
Please?
You like that?
Mathew?
Mathew?

He has drifted into unconsciousness.
 She is desperate now.
 Desperate to keep him warm.
 She tries to pull up some more of the floor.
 It's impossibly hard.
 She gets a splinter of wood and puts it on the fire.
 Then she looks to the doorway.
 She goes to it, comes back.
 Doesn't know what to do.
 She finally makes sure the Boy is safe.
 Then goes out.

SIXTEEN

She stands, looking about, not daring to leave the doorway.

 She sees a stick of wood lying nearby. She rushes to pick it up.

 She is about to return when she sees something else nearby, lying on top of the snow.

 She goes over and picks up a baby's mitten.

 She looks at it. Then she sees something else. It is a soft toy.

 She follows this trail, picking up small things. A baby's things.

 She follows the trail off.

 The Wolf appears. He has been watching her.

SEVENTEEN

Lights up on the kitchen.
    The table.
    The chair.
    The Woman walks in. We are back in the past with
her.
    She is wearing the same clothes, but they are now
clean and normal-looking.
    She looks at the table.
    She sits down.
    The baby-monitor is on the side.
    The light is green.
    She scratches her arm.
    She looks at the pile of baby washing and pulls the
cardigan with the trees from it.
    She looks at one of the knitted trees and then starts to
unpick it.
    She looks up at the glass wall of the box.
    For a moment she seems to see through the wall into
the black forest that is all around it. It is horrible.
    Then she stops herself.
    She goes to the sink and runs the cold water.
    She watches it.
    Then snaps out of it and goes to the cupboard to get
a glass.
    She opens the cupboard and reaches in.
    She pulls her hand out sharply, something has
touched it.
    She looks in.
    She looks.
    Then pulls the glasses out to smash silently on the
floor.
    At the back of the cupboard we see a brown mark on
the plywood.

She pushes it and it gives way.
Her hand goes through.
When she pulls her hand back it is stained dark.
She furiously tries to rub the dark off.
The sound of a baby waking up.
She looks at the baby-monitor.
She looks at the cupboard.
Tries to cover the hole.
But something is coming through. It is dark, maybe the branch of a fir tree.
She tries to wipe her hand clean.
She stares at the baby-monitor.
The light is going red.
She looks at it and turns down the volume.
But the light is still there.
She knocks it to the floor.
But the sound is still there.
She has the cardigan in her hand.
She feels the itch on her arm or collarbone again. She scratches it.
Then it is worse.
She looks at her skin.
It is stained too.
Spreading.
She looks terrified.
She looks at the cardigan.
She leaves the room.

This is when we see our Woman. In the forest.
She has been watching herself.
She has followed the trail here. Her arms are full of the baby things she has collected.
She lets them fall.
She gets closer to the box.
We can see her face lit up.
But she can't get in.
She tries.

She pushes herself against the box.

We hear the crying of a baby.
  We hear the Woman go into the baby's room.
  We hear her say 'Hey', 'Hey'.
  'Look at you. I see you.'
  The baby is picked up and quietens.
  A moment of softness, love, then we hear her intake
of breath, fear.

The Woman in the woods tries to break into the box.
  She can't.
  A sound starts to build in her.
  A keening sound that builds.

We hear the sound of the baby being put back down,
then her voice again:
  'Okay.'
  'Okay.'
  'It'll all be okay.'

The Woman in the woods lets out a cry of grief.

The baby has stopped.
  The baby has been smothered.

EIGHTEEN

The Woman in the woods stops. Dead.
  Feels an enormous pain in her stomach again.
  She doubles over.
  She retches with it.
  She feels the pain again.

The Wolf enters.
  He has some of his old strength back.

Wolf And again.
  And again.

And again.
And again.

She doubles over each time he says it.

And again.
And again.
And again.
And again.

It is like he is kicking her on the floor with his words.

Woman Stop.

Wolf And again.
And again.
And again.
And –

Woman Stop.
Stop!

It stops.
The pain goes.
She is left crumpled.
The Wolf is looking into the kitchen.

Wolf What did it feel like?
His little body?
He wriggle for a bit?
Wriggle. Squirm.

For a bit.

She has had enough.

Okay.

The light of the kitchen goes out and it disappears.
The forest seems to grow thicker. Freezing once more.

(*Gentle.*) Told you.
You gotta leave well alone now.

Right?
You know that, right?

She looks at him.
  Nods.
  He is relieved.

Thought I nearly lost you.
  I thought . . .
  Well . . .
  . . .
  You think you could keep him?
  That little boy?
  Huh?
  You know where that ends up.
  Hell, that ends up right here.
  See, you no good with kids.
  You know that, right?

She nods.

What were you thinking, huh?
  See, now I think of it, it's quite funny.
  You.
  Him.
  I guess it's all quite funny.

Long pause.

Woman Called me Mother.

Wolf What?

Woman In his sleep. I held him one time and he said it.
Mother.

Wolf Do it to me.
  Do it.

He purposely puts himself in her arms.

Like this?

She nods.

You remember when we were like this?

Woman I do.

Wolf You just a girl then.
I would cry so you could hold me.
Course I never really crying. Not really. But I a good actor. I be anything you want me to be.
And you'd tell me one of your stories.
. . .
What's he like?
The boy?

Woman He's so beautiful.
His hair . . .

Wolf Do the voice.

Woman I can't.

Wolf Do the voice.

Woman (*back in her Southern US accent*) It so soft.

The Wolf lets out a sound of wonder.

And he got the most angel face you ever saw.

Wolf Really?
Like a angel?

Woman Like he never did nothing wrong in his whole life.

Wolf Where is he now?

Woman He on the floor.

Wolf Sleeping?

Woman Sleeping.

Wolf You know that's the best thing, don't you?

She nods.

Boys. They trouble.
  They stir things up.

She nods.

I love you.

Woman I know.

Wolf And it's a terrible love I have.
  It's a vicious love.
  But I do love you.
  Even when I'm clawing at you.
  Even when I won't shut up.
  When I cry and cry. I still love you.

Woman (*in a British accent*) You're digging.

Wolf I know.

Woman You're digging in.

Wolf I know.
  . . .
  I'm just reminding you of my love.
  That's the best way.
  Something that hurts.
  No one remember soft things, see.
  No one.
  They remember claws though.
  And they remember scars.
  And teeth.
  And the viciousness.
  They remember that long after everything soft is all
gone away.
  You won't leave me, will you?

She shakes her head.

That's good.
  'Cause I don't think I could take it on my own.
  All the things I remember.
  All the horrible things I done.
  All the nasty things.
  And I only do it for you.
  I only do it because I love you.
  I want you to be proud.
  And that boy.
  He so beautiful.
  He like a angel, ain't he?

  She nods.

But he won't call you Mama.
  Not in real life.
  Not when he find out what you done.
  Only I call you that.
  I'm the only one loves you like that.
  Look at me.
  Look at me.

  She opens her eyes.

'Cause you disgusting.
  You got nothing good inside left at all.
  And I like it.
  I like it when you play hard to get.
  I understand, you need that.
  You want to feel . . . human for a while. Like things
might change, right?
  But they don't.

You and me the same.
  We black as stone at the bottom of a lake.
  We sunk.

You know what you got to do, right?

  She nods.

You bring him to me.
We go back the ways things were.

He leaves.
She gets up.
She looks at the box where the kitchen was, dark now. She can't see in.
She turns from it and walks away.

NINETEEN

Back in the shack.
She is standing over the Boy, who is slumped on the floor.
It is dark.
The fire has one last flame in it.
She looks at the floor and rips up one of the planks.
She stands over him.
She lifts the wood to bring it down on his head.
She can't.

TWENTY

A rising scream.
Lights up.
It is the Wolf.
He is pacing around the walls of the shack.
He stops every so often and screams at her.
It is terrifying.
The floor of the shack has disintegrated. Has been ripped up.
So that the Woman holds the Boy on an island now. The last remains.
The Wolf is a whirlwind of rage.

Wolf You
Give
Him
To
Me.

She holds the Boy.

You
Give
Him
To
Me.

She does not respond.

You.
GIVE
HIM –

His words descend into noise. Scream. Rage.

Fine.
Fine.
You don't like this?
You don't like this world we made here?
You fuck.
You
Fuck.
You
Fuck.
You.
Fuck.

He pulls and pulls on a part of the set.
It comes away.

You wanna do this again, huh?
You wanna make this again, huh?
You wanna.

You think.
You.
You.

He smashes at another piece of the set.
    Destroys it.
    He kicks and smashes and pulls the set down.
    This world.
    He pulls it and rips it apart.

Woman Don't.
    Please.

Wolf Me?
    ME?
    It's not me?
    It's not me, Mama.
    It's not me.
    It's not me.
    YOU
    YOU –

He rages and rips another piece away.

We spinning off, Mama.
    We disappearing.
    Don't you see?
    Don't you see what you're doing?

Woman I don't want to.

Wolf Then
    I say.
    Give him to me.
    Please.

He holds his hands out. Beckoning for the Boy.

Woman I can't.

Wolf Fine.

You be lost then.
See how long you last.

The Wolf pulls the last piece of this world away.
He disappears.

Woman Wait!
Where've you gone?
Where've you gone?

She is left in an empty place.
The Boy wakes up.

Hey. Hey.
It's okay.

Boy What's that?

There is a sound.

Woman Rain.
It's raining.

He has got up.
The fire goes out.
He puts his hands out and feels the rain.

Boy Can we go now?

He collapses into her arms.

She looks at him.

Act Two

ONE

Night.
  She is carrying the Boy.
  The sound of rain.
  The passing of cars.
  Headlights sweep her.
  She is wet through.

Woman Stop!
  Stop!
  Why won't anyone stop?

  The Wolf arrives dressed as a policeman.
    She sees him.
    He is approaching her warily.

Wolf Ma'am.
  Ma'am. It's raining.

Woman Who are you?

Wolf I'm here to help.

Woman Who are you?

Wolf You been here long, ma'am?

Woman . . . I don't know.
  I was looking for help.

Wolf How did you get here?

Woman Walked.

Wolf Long way?

  She nods.

Wolf Boy looks heavy.

Woman He's fine.

Wolf He yours?

She nods.

Only we got a report that someone lost their child.
You see?
The boy there. He fits the description.

Woman Who lost their child?

Wolf A dentist. She's a dentist.
She does me as a matter of fact.

He shows his teeth.

Thought the father was picking him up.
A mix-up.
When she got to school they said he was gone already.
A lady in a light dress.
Would that be you?

Woman No.

Wolf Well, we can discuss that.

Woman She's lying.
Or . . .
She might not be, but this isn't him.

Wolf What's the boy's name?

Woman . . . Mathew.
I think.

Wolf You think?

Woman He's very private.
We're very private.

Wolf Ma'am, I'm going to have to ask you to hand the
boy to me.

Woman Why?

Wolf Because he looks dead, ma'am.

Woman He isn't dead.

Wolf Then you need to help him by handing him over.

Woman No.

Wolf Then I'm afraid we will have to disable you.

Woman What?

Wolf Call in a drone. Neutralise you.

A car goes by, beeping its horn.

Woman Where am I?

Wolf You're on Interstate 617.

Woman Where's that?

Wolf You don't know where you are?
     Ma'am. I'm going to have to ask you to step away
from the edge.

Woman What edge?

Wolf The edge. You're on the edge.
     Can't you see?
     There's a long drop.
     Can't you see that?

She looks down. She is on the edge of a long drop.

Now.
     I'm going to ask you again.
     You need to walk towards me.

Woman What time is it?

Wolf I'm sorry?

Woman The time?
　Do you have the time?

Wolf This really isn't . . .

Woman Why've you not got a watch?
　Huh?
　Are you a law enforcement officer?

Wolf I am.

Woman But you don't have a watch.
　That's unusual.

Wolf It's . . .
　It's being repaired.

Woman By whom?

Wolf . . . A. J. Symmonds Repairs.

Woman Ha!

Wolf What?

Woman There's no such place.

Wolf I can assure you, ma'am –

Woman You got a radio?

Wolf Yes.

Woman Why don't you ask them for the time then?

Wolf This really isn't . . .

Woman What?
　I'm a woman on top of a very high place.
　What is this?
　This a bridge?

Wolf It's a very high bridge.

Woman Over what?
　Rushing water?

Wolf Over concrete.
   You fall.
   You smash into the floor.

Woman That is a very high-risk situation.
   I think that if someone was in that kind of a situation.
   Holding a boy.
   Holding a boy that you seem to think is the son of a
dental hygienist.

Wolf A dentist, ma'am.
   She's fully qualified, ma'am.

Woman Well, if that were the case then I would've
thought you could at least use your radio to find out the
time.

   He looks at her.
      He speaks into his radio.

Wolf Tango Foxtrot Delta. This is Officer Peebles. Come
in please.
   Come in.

   The radio is blank.

Woman Where'd you get that?

Wolf Ma'am.

Woman You been to the fancy dress store?
   It looks cheap, now I see it clearly.
   Look.
   You haven't even got the numbers on right.
   They're all falling off.

   He starts to disintegrate.

You haven't even shaved.
   Nails long.
   Claws all yellow.
   You're bursting out.

Your buttons falling off.
You've just got a cheap costume on.
You think I don't recognise you?
You think that?

Wolf Ma'am.

Woman Where does she live, this dentist?
Is it a nice house?

Wolf It's very nice.

Woman Up on a height somewhere?
Is it called Sunny Heights or something like that?

Wolf Meadow Falls.

Woman Meadow Falls.
And what's it like, this house? Did you visit?

Wolf I had to visit, yes. We always call by in these kind of situations.

Woman She glamorous?
She got a nice body?

Wolf She's not overweight, if that's what you mean.

Woman Guess that's what money does.

Wolf I would certainly say there probably is a link between wealth and obesity. But that doesn't mean you can be fat just because you're poor.
We've all got to try.

Woman Expect she's got a carpet.

Wolf She does.

Woman What colour?

Wolf Cream.

Woman And what? A view?
  Does she have a view?

Wolf It does look out over the ocean, yes.

Woman She barefoot?

Wolf I . . .
  I don't recall.

Woman That's what I'd do.
  If I had that.
  Be barefoot all the time.
  Wouldn't ever go out.
  If I had that soft between my toes.

Wolf Why don't you give the boy to me?

Woman 'Cause I'm not finished yet.
  'Cause I've got to keep him safe. I promised.

Wolf You really think it's cheap?
  The costume?

Woman It's awful.
  Looks like nylon.

Wolf You can't outrun me. Got you surrounded.

Woman Doesn't matter.

Wolf Why not?

Woman 'Cause I'm going to jump.

Wolf You kill him.

Woman I don't think so.

  . . .
  Look.
  I can see it.
  I can still see the trees.
  This is all bullshit.

The car lights disappear.
  She is still in the woods.
  She jumps.
  Black.

TWO

She is in a convenience store, still holding the Boy.
  She looks confused.
  A man is standing behind the checkout, staring at her incredulously.
  On close inspection he looks like the Wolf.

Wolf Yes?
  Yes?
  Madam?
  You are okay?
  Madam?
  You are okay?

Woman Yes.

Wolf You were miles away.

Woman Yes.

Wolf What can I do for you?

Woman I don't know.

Wolf Well, we have a variety of things you can buy.
  Over there is a picnic rug.
  How about that?

Woman Yes.

Wolf It's on offer.
  And also this.

  He pulls out a wicker picnic basket.

It's the kit.
    Look.
    It comes out like this.
    Two glasses.
    Two plates.
    Two knives and forks.
    Two . . .
    Well, two of everything really.
    Are there two of you?

Woman Yes.

Wolf You and the wee one, is it?

Woman Yes.

Wolf Lovely.
    Going somewhere special?
    His favourite beach.
    Watch him play.
    They like that, don't they?
    Rock pools.
    Endless hours.
    Endless hours staring at the waves.
    You've got the kit now.
    You'd look normal.
    What about a costume?
    Do you have something?
    For swimming in.
    Or just for watching.
    You'll need a costume.

He pulls out a whole rack of swimming costumes.

One of these.
    And one of these.
    And one of these.
    And one of these.

Woman What's over there?

Wolf Where?

Woman Over there?

Wolf And one of these.
And one of these.
That's nothing really.
And one of these.
Madam.
And one of these.

Woman There.

Wolf Yes.
Behind the freezer section, do you mean?
That's nothing.
It's a problem actually.
It's nothing to worry about.
The picnic set still works.
The beach will be nice.
Madam?
Madam?

She has started to walk away.

Wait!
. . .
It's an area of outstanding natural beauty.
Designated.
It's very annoying because we have to pay for it.
Pay for them.
I say get rid.
My wife doesn't agree.
I don't have a wife though.
She's dead, I mean.
Are you . . .?
I mean have you . . .?
I mean I don't want to offend anyone.
My remarks.

You have to take them with a pinch of salt.

I'm not against anyone going into the area of outstanding natural beauty.

I suppose they have to.

That's what they say on the news, isn't it?

They say they have to.

They say we don't understand, the people who have to actually work to pay for it.

What I say is maybe if they worked they wouldn't have to stand in it.

Maybe if they worked a bit in this lovely area.

This bit of the shop with the lights.

I mean I'm always looking for a shelf stacker.

I'm always looking for little monkey people to do my bidding.

Stand there.

Do this.

And it's not bad.

I did it.

Why shouldn't *they*?

I had to do it.

I had to pay for it.

I had to work.

I had to work my way up.

And there they are.

Standing in that fucking area of outstanding natural beauty.

Just enjoying it.

I watch them.

I've got a gun.

I've actually got a gun here.

Do you want this too?

I can pop one in if you like.

Free gun with every sale.

What I like to do is train it on one of them.

There they are, just staring.

A lot like yourself.
I mean if you were over there.
You'd look a lot like one.
Just staring.
Looking at God knows what.
They say they need the fresh air.
They need to look at special things.
Like sun, or rain, butterflies. Leaves.
They say they need that.
But what their problem is, they've opened their minds
up too much.
See.
If we all opened our minds up we'd all go fucking
nuts, wouldn't we?
We'd all be standing like gormless fucking cunts.
Gormless fucking useless little scrounging little cunts.
While *I* have to work for it.
While *I* have to –

He has got out a loaded shotgun.
    He goes to aim it at someone in the area of
outstanding natural beauty.

Do you want me to?
    Should I fire?
    It's just a popgun.
    It's just a toy.
    Would you like me to?
    It'd be so easy.
    Would you like me to?
    Would you like to?
    Shall we?
    Shall we?
    Just a little bit.
    Just a little bit of a go.
    Shall we?
    Shall we?

Shall I?
Well?
Well?
It's your choice.
Is this what you want?
Is it?
Is this what you want to go back to?
Well?
Is it?
Well?
Is it?
Look at me.
Look at me!

She looks at him.

Well?
Is that what you want?

He has turned the gun on himself.

Is this what you want?

He has put the barrel in his mouth.
    He looks like he is pleading with her.
    As if she is holding the gun. He is trying to say
'Please, please', but the gun is muffling his words.
    He shoots.
    His brains blow out all over the wall.
    Sirens.
    Black.

THREE

An empty playground.
    The wind blows.
    She arrives. Still carrying the Boy.
    There is a roundabout.

She is exhausted.
She has bloody feet.
She puts the Boy down on the roundabout.

Woman (*calling out*) Hello!
Hello!?

There are two Kids.
One has a Coke can that they chuck away.
They come over.
She looks frightened.

Kid This is our playground.
Did you hear me?
This is our playground.

Woman I just need to rest a minute.

Kid Why you here?
Why you wearing pyjamas?
Why you mad?

Woman I'm not.

Kid Look mad to me.
Doesn't she?

The other Kid laughs.

Can you move this body please?
I want a go on the roundabout.

Woman You're too old.

Kid Don't tell me what I can and can't do.

The Kid stares at her until she moves the Boy.
She goes and puts him on a swing.
The Kid watches all this, then comes over.

Kid I want to use the swing now, please.

Woman There's another one.

Kid This is the one I want to use.

   . . .

   Please.

He stands silent.
   She looks exhausted.
   He stares at her until she moves the Boy to the slide.

I want to use this slide now, please.

Woman You haven't even been on the swing.

Kid I used the swing.

Woman No you didn't.

Kid I did.
   You just didn't see.

Woman . . .

Kid I swang for ages.
   What's wrong with you?
   You got something wrong?

Woman No.

Kid So why did you think I hadn't swung when I had?

Woman I just . . .
   I thought you just looked at it, then came over here.

Kid (*to the other Kid*) Did I just look at the swing?

The other Kid laughs.

See.

Woman What?
   He just laughed.
   He didn't say anything.

Kid Why the fuck are you here?
   Why the fuck are you always here?

Dragging that thing around.
You looking to pick up?

Woman No.

Kid I cum in your mouth if you want.
But that's it.
I ain't letting you touch me.

Woman I just need a rest.

Kid Well, you can't rest here.

Woman It's a public place.

Kid It's ours.
Don't you see that?
You don't belong here.
Unless you want to go on the swing?

She shakes her head.

(*To the other Kid.*) Did you see that?
Unless you want a go on the swing, I said.

The other Kid laughs.

Woman Stop it.

Kid What?

Woman (*angry now*) Stop it.

The other Kid laughs.

Kid (*to the other Kid*) She is after you.
You better be afraid.

The Kid laughs.

Woman Stop laughing.
You hear me?
Stop laughing.

The Kid laughs.

She goes to slap him.
He grabs her and twists her.
They dance.
It is out of control.
Sometimes she is with him, sometimes alone.
Finally, she falls to her knees.
The Kid steps away and watches.

Kid Open your mouth.

She refuses.
   Then her mouth is forced open.
   She gags as she feels fingers being forced into her mouth.
   The Kid is almost gone.

Now say sorry.
   Sorry for what you did.

She has stopped struggling.

Say it.

She tries to say sorry, but she still feels fingers in her mouth.

Again.

She tries again.

Again.

She twists and falls to the ground.

Ground not good enough for you?
   Is that it?

Alone, she sees the Boy and moves to hold him.
   A Woman with a pushchair arrives.
   It is the Wolf dressed up.
   She is smoking.

Wolf That those boys again?
  They're terrible, aren't they?
  Here.
  I'll help you up.
  Oh, they have a terrible cheek.
  Did they punch you?
  They're always punching people.
  They don't mean anything by it.
  Cigarette?

She shakes her head.

Good.
  Yes.
  Good.
  Terrible habit.
  I should stop really, but then I think, I can't. I don't
have the willpower. I'll just die a terrible death. Isn't that
awful?
  Are you local?

Woman I'm . . .

Wolf What?
  Speak up, dear.

Woman I'm trying to get back.

Wolf Back where?

Woman I don't know.

Wolf Sound like you don't know much at all.
  Letting them boys all over you.

Woman I didn't.

Wolf Course.
  (*Noticing her cigarette.*) Look at that.
  I've barely smoked at all.
  Look at that ash, hanging there?

That's about to fall, isn't it?
That's disgusting really.
All that in your lungs.
I don't know why we do it.
But we do.
You've not really said much.
What?
What is it?
Are you tired?

She nods.

You should just fall asleep. That's what I do.
    Middle of the day.
    Any time really.
    I wake up in the strangest places.
    Upside down.
    Hanging off things.
    Covered in my own vomit once or twice.
    It's so dark, isn't it?
    These nights.
    They're so dark.

She looks at the Boy.

Oh, it's him, is it?
    You looking after him, are you?
    Go on. You could just leave him if you want.
    You could.
    No one would notice.
    He'd just be swept up by the sweeping machine.
    They're very clean here.

Indicating the buggy.

I can see you looking at the wee one.
    Would you like a little look?
    Go on.
    Pick him up.

That's fine.
Go on.
He likes to be picked up.

She puts the Boy down and picks up the baby from the pram.

Would you like to feed him?
He likes to be fed.
Look at him.
Little tyke.
Would you like him?
You'd have to think of a name, of course.
What would you call him?

Woman Mathew.

Wolf Mathew.
That's a good name.
Course you'd have to promise to look after him.
Can you promise that?
Can you?
Can you?

The Woman nods, looking at the little baby.

There there.
There there.
There there.
Oh, you're –
Is that –?
Oh dear.
Oh whoopsie.
Oh dear.
Oh dear.
Oh dearie me.

The Woman looks at herself. There is a black stain spreading out across her dress.
She looks at the baby in her arms.

It has gone, leaving her hands black with something.
She tries to wipe it off.
She looks for the Boy. He has gone.
She searches for him.

Woman Mathew.
Mathew.
Mathew.
MATHEW!

The Wolf is frantic now.
Running round the space after her.
Taunting her.
Making faces at her.
She has to push him out of the way.
Finally she is exhausted and they face each other.
The Kid from earlier comes on now, dressed as a
hospital porter.
He takes her away.

FOUR

A bright light.
She is in a clean place.
Sitting on a chair.
She has been given a white gown.
The Wolf has changed.
He has a pen in the pocket of his shirt and a file.
He sits opposite her.

Wolf Better?

Woman Sorry?

Wolf Feeling any better?
Had a little wobble there.

Woman Yes.
Thank you.

I'm sorry . . .
Where am I?

Wolf You're in St Joseph's.
You remember . . .?

Woman . . . Yes.

Wolf Good.

. . .
Right, well, we've had all the bloods back and you'll
be pleased to know that there seems to be nothing
wrong.

Woman Right.

Wolf Of course. The drugs you're on. They could easily
account for the confusion.

Woman I see.

Wolf We'll keep you in, just routine.

Woman How long?

Wolf Oh, probably just a few days.
Is that okay?

She nods.

Woman What about –

She stops herself.

Wolf What about what?

Woman . . . Nothing.

Wolf Are you sure?

She nods.
He looks at her, then writes a note on his
clipboard.

Woman What are you writing?

Wolf Just a note.

74

Woman About me?

Wolf Yes.

Woman What?

Wolf Well, just . . .

Woman What?

Wolf Well, just that there still seem to be some issues.

Woman Why? Why have you written that?

Wolf Look. It's just a precaution.
We're here to keep an eye on you
We're here for your own good.
You don't want to end up in . . .

Woman What?

Wolf Well, we don't want you distressed.

Woman An area of outstanding natural beauty?

Wolf Sorry?

Woman You don't want me in an area of outstanding
natural beauty.

Wolf I don't know what you're talking about.

Woman Rub it out.

Wolf I'm sorry?
. . .
I can't. It's pen.

Woman Then cross it out.

Wolf We can't cross out notes.
Not once they're down.
They stay.

Woman Just . . .
I didn't say anything.

Wolf I think you did.

Woman No.

Wolf You were going to ask me a question.

Woman No.

Wolf See. There it is. It's still there, isn't it?

Woman It's not.

Wolf It is. I can see your lips trembling.

Woman No.

Wolf I'm sorry. I'm going to have to write more notes now.

Woman What about?

Wolf Your lips trembling.
   Your ears moving.
   You're upset.

Woman I'm not.

Wolf You are.

Woman I'm not.
   I'm not.

   He continues to write.

Please. Please stop.

Wolf Could you just look at the pen for me?
   Could you just look left and right for me?
   Could you just tell me how you feel?
   Could you tell me how this feels?
   Does this hurt?
   Does this hurt?
   How about here?

   She winces.

Still a problem?

Woman No.

Wolf I think there is.

Woman No.

Wolf Are we going to have to restrain you?

Woman No.

Wolf Because you look like you might be distressed. And we know where distress leads.

Woman No.

Wolf Because that's the look you always do when you're distressed.
    Always do.
    It's your tell, really.
    If you were playing poker that would be how we'd beat you.
    Every time.
    Because you can't really control it, can you?
    You can't really control.

He has restrained her.
    She tries to struggle.
    The lights dim.
    She struggles.

Woman Let me out.
    Please.
    Let me out.

The lights are turned out.
    We realise she's still in the woods.
    Darkness.

FIVE

And there in the dark.
  She hears him.
  The Boy walks in. He can't see her.

Woman Mathew?
  Stop.

Boy Yes.

Woman Wait.
  Stop.
  Wait.

  She pulls against her restraints.

Boy I thought you'd gone.

Woman No.

Boy I thought you'd left me.

  He falls to the floor.
  She breaks free of her restraints.
  She finds and holds him.

I'm sorry.

Woman Shhhh.

Boy I'm sorry I wasn't what you wanted.

Woman You were.
  You were all I wanted.

Boy Tell me.

Woman . . . What?

Boy Tell me about me.
  I can't.
  I don't remember it.

  . . .

  I was born . . .

Woman You were born.

Boy Early.

Woman Yes.

   . . .

Boy Tell me.

Woman . . .
   It was early.
   Could see the sky. Ward must've been high up.
   Line of light.
   Sun not even up.
   And I found you there.
   In my arms.
   This thing.
   Chewing.
   Mouth chewing.
   Hand . . . clutching.
   And I felt so . . .
   Like I was looking out of someone else's body.
   This woman.
   This thing chewing on her.
   Sky going blue now.
   Must've been a sunny day.

People look at you.
   You look at them.
   You have this thing with you.
   People say 'Oh'
   And 'Ah, you must be so . . .'
   You must be so . . .
   Jealous some
   And others nothing
   And others feeling the same.
   Could see those ones.
   The ones feeling the same.
   Like . . . 'What's happening to me?'
   'Why don't I feel . . .'

Day.
And night.
And day.
Milk.
And radiators on.
And all these people.
And all these nights when I'm just . . .
I get further away.
Notice I'm in someone else's body more and more.
And where *I* am . . .?
Well, I look about and there's these things.
Sprouting up.
All around.
In this place where *I* am. Where I really am.
The tops of trees.
And I can see them, fully formed. Coming up out of
the ground. In this place.
This strange place.
And I'm afraid.
'Help!'
'Help!'
No one hears.
Because of course I'm not making a sound.
This body I'm in. I can't make it even make a sound.
She just plods on.
Feeding.
And walking.
And looking at all those people.
While the trees are growing up.
Getting thicker.
Until the branches are clawing at you and pulling and
all you can see is needles and the feel of that.
The crushing feel of that.
I thought I was dying.
And then . . .
I'm there.

I'm there.
Room.
Quiet.
Dark.
Just the glow from the baby-monitor.
Someone's done all this. This room. A child's room.
The crack of light under the door.
Sound from the TV downstairs.
And I'm here.
I'm actually here.
And the relief.
No forest. No trees.
It's dark, but I can see his cot in the corner.
And it seems good.
Yes.
It seems good.
This cot in the corner.
And I think.
I'm okay.
I'm okay.
And I go over to lift him.
Him.
The weight of him.
This sleeping softness.
This overwhelming softness.
This breath.
This breath and love and warmth.
This beautiful thing.
And I . . .
And I . . .
I . . .
I wish
I wish
I want I want I want I want to stay there.
But ohhhhhhhh –

She lets out a sound of pain.

I can't.
Because that's when I see.
I see it growing in you.
This dark.
This thing already got to you.
This awful thing you got from me.
And it's growing in you and I want . . .
I want not.
But I can't.
I can't have it.
And so I put you down.
And I take your blanket.
And I put it over your face.
And tell you okay.
I tell you okay.
I tell you it'll all be okay.
I did that.
I did that.

She can't look at him. He takes her hand. She looks at him.

Boy Thought you'd left me.

Woman No.
. . .
You can stand?

Boy I think . . .
I think I can't.

Woman Then I'll carry you.

Boy No.

Woman Then I'll carry you.

Boy No.

Woman Then I'll carry you.
    Please.

Boy No

Woman Let me carry you?

Boy No.

Woman Let me . . .

Boy No.

Woman Then what?

Boy You see?

Woman What?

Boy You see?

   There is a light. It starts to fill the whole stage.

Woman What is it?

Boy Life.

   She sees.

I remember when you found me.

Woman What?

Boy When you dug me from the snow.
    I was a strange lump.
    You found me.

   She nods.

I'm glad you found me.
    It was no fun.
    In the storm.
    Thought I was alone.
    But I heard your voice.
    You were calling me, weren't you?

   She nods.

Thought so.

. . .
Mathew!
Mathew.

. . .

. . .
Mum.

He dies.
> *She picks him up and starts to walk to the light.*
> *The Wolf arrives.*
> *He looks different. Calm.*
> *She tries to get past him with the Boy.*
> *But he won't let her.*

Wolf Just you.
Alone.

She gives up the Boy to him.
> *She leaves.*

Bye then.
Oh it's been so nice.
Oh it's been so fine.
Why yes.
Why yes of course.
Of course we must.

. . .
See you later . . . alligator.
In a while . . . crocodile.

The Wolf looks at the Boy. He hugs him close.
> *Black.*

SIX

Black.
> *The sound of birds.*
> *The sounds of the woods.*

The End.

84